Website

Designing

A comprehensive guide on creating a website from basics

By

John M. Sterling

Table of Content

Introduction

Introductions establish the tone for a written or spoken piece. In essays, speeches, and presentations, the introduction gives context and history, underlines the purpose or thesis statement, and engages the audience. A good beginning may hook the audience, set the tone, and guide the rest of the work.

Business Websites' Significance

Nowadays, your business needs a website. Reasons:

1. Internet Presence: A website gives your firm 24/7 online visibility. This lets potential clients locate you and learn about your products or services anytime, anywhere.

2. Credibility: A professional website can boost your business's legitimacy. A well-designed and comprehensive website can also increase client trust.

3. Marketing: Websites can reach more people than traditional marketing tactics. Your website can display your products and

services, publish client testimonials, and educate your target audience.

4. Competitive Advantage: In today's competitive business market, having a website might provide you an edge over competitors without one. It can increase search engine rankings and customer acquisition.

5. Consumer Convenience: A website lets customers locate information, place orders, and pay online.

Business websites are essential to digital marketing. It can boost your credibility, audience, and customer convenience.

Business Websites

Businesses can use numerous sorts of websites for marketing their products or services, communicating with customers, and building their online presence. Common business websites:

1. Corporate Websites: These are the most typical business websites, including information about the company, its history, mission, products or services, and contact information. Large enterprises, professional service firms, and non-profits use them.

2. E-Commerce Websites: They are for internet retailers. Customers can buy straight from these sites using product catalogs, shopping carts, and payment gateways.

3. Portfolio Websites: Photographers, graphic designers, and painters utilize portfolio websites to acquire clients. These sites have galleries, contact information, and client testimonials.

4. Blog Websites: Businesses utilize blog websites to enhance their brand, provide regular content, and establish industry authority. Articles, news, and other relevant stuff populate these sites.

5. Landing Pages: Single-page websites that convert visitors into leads or customers. They are used for advertising, special promotions, and visitor contact information.

6. Social Media Websites: Facebook, Twitter, LinkedIn, and Instagram allow businesses to engage with customers and advertise their products and services through social media marketing.

Goals, industry, and the audience will determine a business's website. It's crucial to choose a website that meets your business goals and effectively conveys your message.

Business Website Essentials

Every business website needs certain elements to reach its audience and fulfill its goals. Key elements:

1. Homepage: Visitors land on your homepage. It should summarize your business and offerings.

2. About Us: Include your company's history, mission, beliefs, and team on this page. This page can develop trust and credibility.

3. Products/Services: Your Products/Services page should detail your offerings. This page should showcase your product's features and benefits using high-quality photographs and videos.

4. Testimonials: Satisfied consumers can develop credibility and confidence with new customers. Social proof from customer evaluations and testimonials on your website can attract new customers.

5. Contact Information: Your website should include clear phone, email, and physical addresses. Visitors can contact you easily via a contact form.

6. Blog: A blog on your website can boost your credibility and add value to your audience. It can boost traffic and search engine rankings.

7. Calls-to-Action (CTAs): "Contact Us," "Purchase Now," and "Subscribe" can help website visitors take the required action. Clear CTAs can boost website conversions and help you reach your business goals.

These basic website elements can help you develop an online presence, reach your target audience, and achieve your business goals.

Chapter 1

Planning and Preparation

Business websites need planning and preparation. Key considerations:

Then, define your website's aims. What is your website's goal? Do you want more leads, sales, or brand recognition online? Goals will guide website design and development.

2. Know Your Target Audience: A website that effectively connects with potential customers requires knowing your target audience. To guarantee your website resonates with your target audience, consider age, gender, geography, interests, and shopping behaviors.

3. Analyze your competitor's websites to see what works. To stand out in your sector, study their design, content, and functionality.

4. Select Your Platform: WordPress, Squarespace, and Wix are website platforms. Choose the platform that fits your needs and budget.

5. Make a Site Map: A site map shows your website's structure and content. It can help visitors navigate your website.

6. Create a Content Strategy: Your website's material should be interesting, useful, and targeted. Create a content plan that specifies the sorts of material, frequency, and authors.

7. Choose a Design: Your website's design should be attractive, user-friendly, and brand-consistent. Choose a design that conveys your brand's values.

8. Test and Launch: Before launching your website, test it for bugs and functionality. Launch and market your website when you're happy.

Business websites require planning and preparation. Define your goals, target audience, platform, site map, and content strategy, and design, test, and launch your website.

Setting Website Goals

Successful business websites start with setting goals and objectives. Key considerations:

1. Set Company Goals: Start with your business objectives. What is your website's goal? Do you want more leads, sales, or brand recognition online? Website design and development are guided by corporate goals.

2. Establish Website Objectives: After identifying your business goals, set website objectives. Generate leads, and your goals can be to increase website traffic by 50% in six months or form submissions by 25% in a quarter.

3. Evaluate Your Target Audience: Your website's goals and objectives should match your target audience's preferences. To guarantee your website resonates with your target audience, consider age, gender, geography, interests, and shopping behaviors.

4. Choose Key Performance Indicators (KPIs): These metrics will measure your website's success. Track KPIs that match your aims to ensure progress.

5. Prioritize Your Objectives: Your business goals and target audience may need you to prioritize your aims. Prioritize your goals.

6. Make an Action Plan: After setting website goals and objectives, make an action plan to attain them. Your action plan should include tasks, deadlines, and stakeholders.

Define your website goals and objectives to create a website that connects with your target audience and meets your company goals. Set business goals, make clear and quantifiable targets, analyze your target audience, choose KPIs, prioritize your objectives, and create an action plan.

Targeting

Successful business websites start with audience identification. Key considerations:

Define your ideal consumer first. To profile your target audience, consider age, gender, location, interests, and shopping behaviors.

2. Market Research: Study your target audience to learn more. To understand their needs, preferences, and behaviors, analyze demographic and psychographic data.

3. Identify Pain Points: Determine your audience's pain points and issues. Knowing their issues helps you create relevant content and features.

4. Assess Your Competition: See how your competitors target the same audience on their websites. Find your niche by identifying what works and what doesn't.

5. User Experience: Consider user experience when designing your website. Make your website accessible to disabled visitors, easy to navigate, and fast. Create target audience personals.

Personals should comprise demographics, behaviors, motivations, and pain points.

7. Test Your Website: Get usability, content, and design input from your target audience. Utilize this input to develop and better serve your audience.

Identifying your target demographic is crucial to building a website that engages potential buyers. Define your target consumer, conduct market research, discover pain points, study your competitors, consider user experience, create personas, and test your website. Understanding your target audience helps you build a website that converts.

Branding

Business websites need a strong brand identity. Key considerations:

Start with brand values. What are your company's values? What distinguishes you? Determine your brand's mission, vision, and values.

2. Brand Audit: Assess your branding efforts through a brand audit. Make sure your logo, colors, font, and messaging match your brand values and target demographic.

3. Establish a Brand Style Guide: Outline your brand's visual and messaging principles. Logo, color palette, typography, tone of voice, and messaging approach.

4. Create a Brand-Reflective Website Design: Utilize your brand style guide to construct your website. Make sure your website is attractive, user-friendly, and in line with your brand.

5. Consistent Content: Develop brand-aligned material. Create engaging content using your brand's voice and message plan.

6. Employ Brand-Related Images and Graphics: Photos, illustrations, and infographics can convey your marketing message.

7. Monitor and Adapt Your Brand: Adjust your brand identity as needed. Your brand identity may change as your firm does.

Business websites need a strong brand identity. Define your brand values, conduct a brand audit, build a brand style guide, design your website, provide consistent content, use imagery and graphics, and monitor and evolve your brand. You may build brand trust and recognition by building a consistent and engaging brand identity.

Competitor Research

Successful company websites require competitor research. Key considerations:

Identify your competition first. See similar businesses that compete for the same audience.

2. Study Their Websites: Check out your competitor's websites to discover how they're positioning their brand, what they're selling, and how they're engaging with customers. Examine their website design, UX, and content.

3. Assess Their Content: Examine your competitors' material to determine how they engage their audience. Find their strengths and ways to stand out.

4. Find Important Features: Find your competitors' website's essential features. Look for aspects that resonate with their

audience and evaluate how you might offer comparable or unique features to set them apart.

5. Evaluate Their SEO Strategy: Check your competitors' search engine rankings by analyzing their SEO approach. Check their keywords, backlinks, and on-page optimization.

6. Monitor Social Media: See how your competitors engage with their audience on social media. Create engaging content, interact with your audience, and connect with potential consumers.

7. Find Opportunities: Finally, find ways to stand out from the competition. Think about customer service, distinctive products, and great user experience.

Successful company websites require competitor research. Identify your competitors, examine their websites and content, identify essential features, analyze their SEO approach, monitor social media, and seek ways to differentiate. Understanding your competition helps you create a website that differentiates your brand.

Chapter 2

Development and Design

Business websites need design and development. Key considerations:

1. Pick Your Platform: Choose a platform that meets your business aims. Consider usability, customization, and scalability.

Start by wireframing and prototyping your website design. Before starting construction, you must design and test your website's layout and structure.

3. Build Your Website: Use best practices for website design and development. This involves making your site quick, safe, and mobile-friendly.

4. Content Creation: Develop engaging, brand-aligned content. Text, photos, and other multimedia content promoting your products or services.

5. SEO: Optimize your website for search engines using SEO best practices. This covers keyword optimization, backlink strategy, and website structure optimization.

6. User Testing: Utilize real users to improve your website. This entails gathering target audience feedback, assessing user behavior, and implementing website design and content changes.

7. Launch and Maintenance: Launch and maintain your website. Updates, security checks, and website optimization are included.

Business website design and development are essential. Take the time to identify the ideal platform, wireframe and prototype your design, develop your website using best practices, generate interesting content, implement SEO best practices, test your website with users, and manage it over time. You may lead your industry by creating a website that meets your business goals and engages your audience.

Domain and Hosting Selection

Successful company websites start with domain names and web hosting. Key considerations:

1. Selecting a Domain Name: Your domain name is your website's address. Consider branding, memorability, and business relevancy while picking a domain name. Choose a short, easy-to-pronounce domain name.

2. Registering Your Domain Name: After choosing your domain name, register it. Domain registration online usually requires an annual fee.

3. Selecting Web Hosting: Web hosting lets you store and publish your website files on a server. Consider uptime, speed, security, and support when choosing a web host.

4. Web Hosting: Shared, dedicated, and cloud web hosting are available. Depending on your business objectives and budget, each style offers pros and cons.

5. Selecting a Hosting Provider: After choosing a hosting type, find a provider with the features and support you need. Choose a

supplier that guarantees uptime, fast loading speeds, and responsive customer assistance.

6. Domain Name and Hosting Setup: After registering your domain name and picking a hosting provider, set up your domain name and a hosting account. This entails uploading your website files and pointing your domain name to your hosting provider's servers.

Domain names and web hosting are crucial to a successful business website. Choose a domain and web host. that match your brand and are easy to remember. By choosing the right domain name and web hosting provider, you can build a trustworthy online presence for your business and make your website accessible to your target audience.

Website Platform and CMS Selection

A business website's platform and CMS are crucial. Key considerations:

1. Website Platform: A website platform powers your website. WordPress, Shopify, Squarespace, Wix, and others are website platforms. Consider website platform ease of use, customization, scalability, and security.

2. CMS: A CMS lets you manage website content. CMSs are available separately or built into most website platforms. Consider ease of use, content production and editing, and software integration when picking a CMS.

3. Customization Options: Choose a website platform and CMS that meets your business demands and ambitions. This covers website design, content creation, and integration with other software.

4. Scalability: Choose a website platform and CMS that scales. Ensure sure the CMS can handle more material and users as your business grows.

5. Security: Choose a secure CMS and platform. SSL encryption and frequent security upgrades and fixes are included.

6. Support and Documentation: Pick a website platform and CMS with trustworthy support and documentation. Customer assistance, community forums, knowledge bases, tutorials, and tips for getting started and troubleshooting are included.

Choosing a platform and CMS for your business website is crucial. Consider your business objectives and goals and choose a platform and CMS with customization, scalability, security, and support. Use the proper platform and CMS to design a website that engages your target audience, supports your business goals, and boosts your online presence

Sitemaps and Wireframes

Website design and development require site maps and wireframes. Know this:

1. Site Map: A site map shows your website structure. It displays page relationships. Site maps manage content and navigation. It helps your staff and stakeholders understand your website structure.

2. Website page wireframes: They just reveal the page layout, not color or graphics. Wireframes plan the user experience and position key features on each page. Before investing in design and development, they help stakeholders provide feedback.

3. Site map and wireframe tools: Sketch, Figma, XD, and Balsamiq are popular. Many internet platforms include a site map and wireframe capabilities.

4. Site Maps and Wireframes: To make your website intuitive and user-friendly, adopt best practices while designing site maps and wireframes. This involves structuring content logically, making navigation clear and consistent, and highlighting crucial features like calls to action on each page. Site maps and wireframes should also take into account your target audience's preferences.

Website design and development require site maps and wireframes. They organize material, plan navigation, and make your website user-friendly. To streamline website design and development, build a site map and wireframes for each page.

Web layout and UI design

Website layout and UI design are essential. Key considerations:

1. Branding: Your website should reflect your company's values and messaging. Create a memorable design using your brand colors, fonts, and pictures.

2. User Experience (UX): Your website style and UI should make it easy for visitors to find what they need and take action. Examine navigation, page structure, and call-to-action placement.

3. Mobile Optimization: More people are using smartphones and tablets to access the internet; thus, your website should be suited for them. Your design should respond to the device's screen size.

4. Accessibility: Your website design should accommodate disabled people. To make your website accessible, consider color contrast, font size, and image alt text.

5. White Space: Utilize white space to freshen up your design. White space organizes content and makes your website easier to explore.

6. Consistency: Employ consistent colors, fonts, and layouts throughout your website for a professional look. Consistency also simplifies website navigation.

7. Testing: Get user input on your website design. This might help you find and fix issues before releasing your website.

Designing a website style and user interface involves numerous elements. You may design a website that expresses your brand and supports your business goals by addressing user experience, mobile optimization, accessibility, and other factors.

Website Writing

Business websites need content. Website writing tips:

1. Know Your Audience: Know who visits your website and what they want. Create material that directly meets their needs and interests.

2. Keep It Simple: Speak clearly. Avoid jargon and technical terminology.

Benefits: Concentrate on product advantages rather than characteristics. Show how your products can help customers.

4. Employ Keywords: Utilize relevant keywords throughout your website content to increase SEO and help potential clients find you online.

5. Be Unique: Create material that differentiates you from the competition. Copying content from other websites might impact SEO and reputation.

6. Make It Scannable: Use subheadings, bullet points, and short paragraphs to make your content easier to scan and find.

7. Calls-to-Action: Add calls-to-action across your website to encourage users to act. This includes joining up for a newsletter or buying something.

8. Proofread and Edit: Check your website material for errors and professionalism.

Writing good company website content is crucial. Content that drives traffic and turns visitors into customers may be created by analyzing your target, emphasizing product benefits, and employing keywords.

Chapter 3

Creating

Company websites need design and development. Priorities:

1. Select Your Platform: Choose a platform that suits your business goals. Usability, personalization, and scalability.

Wireframe and prototype your website design. Design and test your website's layout and structure before building.

3. Design and Develop Your Website: Employ best practices. Make your site fast, safe, and mobile-friendly.

Content Production: Create brand-relevant content. Promotional text, images, and video.

5. SEO: SEO-optimize your website. Keyword, backlink, and website structure optimization.

6. User Testing: Improve your website with real users. This involves target audience feedback, user behavior analysis, and website design and content adjustments.

Launch and maintain your website. Website optimization, security, and updates are included.

Company website design and development are crucial. Choose the right platform, wireframe and prototype your design, develop your website using best practices, create engaging content, implement SEO best practices, test your website with users, and manage it over time. A website that matches your business goals and engages your audience might lead your sector.

Domain/Hosting Choice

Domain names and hosting start successful company websites. Priorities:

1. Domain Name Selection: Your domain name is your website's address. Domain names should reflect branding, memorability, and business relevance. Pick a brief, pronounceable domain name.

2. Registering Your Domain Name: Register it after picking it up. Online domain registration costs per year.

3. Web Hosting: A server stores and publishes your website files. Web hosts should provide uptime, speed, security, and support.

Web hosting: Shared, dedicated, and cloud. Each style has perks and cons depending on business goals and budget.

5. Choosing a Hosting Provider: After picking a hosting type, find a provider with the capabilities and assistance you require. Select a supplier with uptime, fast loading, and responsive customer service.

After registering your domain name and choosing a hosting provider, set up your domain name and a hosting account. Upload your website files and point your domain name to your hosting provider's servers.

Business websites need domain names and hosting. Pick an easy-to-remember domain and web host. You may establish trust and make your website accessible to your target audience by picking the correct domain name and web hosting company.

Website Platform/CMS Choosing

Business websites need platforms and CMS. Priorities:

1. Website Platform: Website platforms power websites. Website systems include Shopify, Squarespace, Wix, and WordPress. Evaluate website platform usability, customization, scalability, and security.

2. CMS: Website content management. Most website systems offer CMSs. Choose a CMS based on the simplicity of use, content development and editing, and software integration.

3. Customization Options: Pick a website platform and CMS that suits your business goals. Website design, content creation, and software integration are included.

Scalability: Choose a scalable website platform and CMS. Verify the CMS can manage more content and users as your organization grows.

5. Secure CMS and platform. SSL encryption and periodic security patches are included.

6. Support and Documentation: Choose a CMS and platform with reliable support and documentation. Customer support, community forums, knowledge bases, tutorials, and starting and troubleshooting instructions are available.

Business website platforms and CMS are vital. Choose a platform and CMS that supports customization, scalability, security, and business needs. Design a website that engages your audience, supports your business goals, and enhances your online visibility using the right platform and CMS.

Sitemaps

Website development requires site maps and wireframes. Know:

1. Site Map: A site map reveals the website structure. Displays page relationships. Sitemaps organize material and navigation. It clarifies the website structure for staff and stakeholders.

2. Webpage wireframes: They show page layout, not color or graphics. Wireframes organize page features and user experience. They gather stakeholder feedback before designing and developing.

3. Sitemap and wireframe tools: Sketch, Figma, XD, and Balsamiq are popular. Several websites have site maps and wireframes.

4. Site Maps/Wireframes: Site maps and wireframes should follow best practices for ease of use. This involves organizing content logically, simplifying navigation, and emphasizing key elements like calls to action on each page. Site maps and wireframes should consider your audience's preferences.

Website development requires site maps and wireframes. They organize content, plan navigation, and simplify your website. Site maps and page wireframes simplify website design and development.

UI/web design

Web design and Interface are crucial. Priorities:

1. Branding: Your website should communicate your company's ideals. Using your brand colors, fonts, and images, develop something unforgettable.

2. User Experience (UX): Your website's design and UI should help visitors find and act. Check navigation, page structure, and CTA placement.

3. Mobile Optimization: Increasingly, people are utilizing smartphones and tablets to access the internet; therefore, your website should be mobile-friendly. Design for screen size.

4. Accessibility: Design your website for impaired individuals. Color contrast, font size, and image alt text make a website accessible.

5. White Space: White space refreshes design. White space simplifies webpage navigation.

6. Consistency: Use consistent colors, fonts, and layouts throughout your website to look professional. Consistency simplifies website navigation.

7. Test your website design with users. This may help you detect and fix website bugs before launch.

Website design and user interface involve many factors. User experience, mobile optimization, accessibility, and other aspects can help you build a website that communicates your brand and supports your company goals.

Web Writing

Company websites need content. Website writing tips: Know your audience and what they desire. Make content for them.

2. Talk plainly. Avoid technical language.

Product benefits, not features. Demonstrate your items' benefits.

4. Use Keywords: Use important keywords throughout your website content to boost SEO and help clients locate you online.

5. Be Unique: Make content that sets you apart. Copying content from other sites may hurt SEO and reputation.

6. Make It Scannable: Subheadings, bullet points, and brief paragraphs make the text easier to skim and find.

7. Calls-to-Action: Encourage users to act through calls-to-action on your website. This includes purchasing or subscribing.

8. Proofread and edit: Make sure your website is professional.

Good firm website content is essential. Analyzing your target, stressing product benefits, and using keywords can generate traffic and buyers.

Chapter 4

Launch and Maintenance

The website launch is just the start. After your website launches, you must make sure it runs well and meets customer needs. Business website launch and maintenance tips:

1. Complete a launch checklist before launching your website. Test your website, check for broken links, optimize content, and set up analytics and monitoring tools.

2. Launch Promotion: Tell your consumers and followers about your website debut. This can attract customers.

3. Website Maintenance: Your website needs regular maintenance to stay secure, up-to-date, and functional. Update software, check website performance, and back up data.

4. Frequent Content Updates: Fresh material can boost search engine rankings, traffic, and customer engagement. New products, blog entries, and website text are examples.

5. Analytics Tracking: Monitor website performance and visitor activity with Google Analytics. This might help you improve and evaluate your website.

6. Consumer Feedback: Request website comments on usability, content, and functionality. This can help you develop your website and satisfy customer expectations.

7. Security Updates: Periodically update your website software, including plugins and themes, to prevent vulnerabilities.

8. Backup Your Website: Back up your website data regularly in case of a crash or other technical difficulties.

In conclusion, building and maintaining your business website demands constant attention. These recommendations will help your website work effectively, meet consumer needs, and develop your business.

Website Testing

Testing your website before launch ensures that everything works and that visitors have a good experience. Check these areas:

1. Functionality: Check all website functions, including forms, shopping carts, and other interactive aspects.

2. Website navigation: Make sure it's simple. Visitors should locate what they need and navigate your site without difficulty.

3. Mobile Responsiveness: Test your website on smartphones and tablets to make sure it looks fine on all screen sizes.

4. Browser Compatibility: Check your website's compatibility and appearance in Chrome, Firefox, Safari, and Internet Explorer.

5. Speed and Performance: Use Google, PageSpeed, Insights, or GTmetrix to test website speed and performance. Make sure your website loads swiftly and has no broken links.

6. Content Accuracy: Verify spelling, grammar, and links on your website.

7. User Testing: Test your website's usability and functionality with a small group. Before releasing your site, this can assist you in finding places for improvement.

Testing your website ensures that it is functional, user-friendly, and optimized for a good user experience. This can boost audience trust and business website success.

Website Launch

Launching your website is thrilling, but it requires planning to go smoothly. Launching a business website requires these steps:

1. Double-Check Everything: Before releasing your website, verify all content, links, and functionality. Make sure your website works on all devices and browsers.

2. Choose a Launch Date: Give yourself ample time to finalize your website launch. Launch during a slack period to avoid overburdening your team and give you time to resolve concerns.

3. Announce Your Launch: Tell your customers and followers about your website debut on social media, email newsletters, and other marketing platforms. This can boost traffic and brand awareness.

4. Monitor Performance: After launch, monitor website performance. Monitor website traffic, bounce rate, and other metrics to spot issues and make modifications.

5. Updates: Schedule software, security, and content updates for your website. This will help your website run well and meet user needs.

Establishing your website is a great business milestone, but it demands careful planning and attention to detail. Follow these steps to launch your business successfully online.

Monitoring Website Traffic

Monitoring and analyzing website traffic is crucial to understanding its performance and user behavior. Tracking and analyzing website traffic involves several steps:

1. Track traffic with Google Analytics. To track page views, user behavior, and other information, add the tracking code to every page.

2. Establish Goals: Use your analytics program to track website actions like purchases and contact form submissions. This can help you optimize your website.

3. Analyze User Behavior: Understand how website visitors interact with your content by analyzing user behavior. Bounce rate, duration on site, and pageviews indicate which pages are functioning well and which require improvement.

4. Track Traffic Sources: Know where your website visitors are coming from. Referral, search, and social traffic might reveal your site's top visitor sources.

5. Adjust: Utilize analytics to make website changes. Improve user experience, SEO, and conversions.

Monitoring and analyzing website traffic takes constant attention. Web analytics tools and traffic statistics can help you make informed decisions about your website and enhance its performance over time.

Website Upkeep

Maintaining and updating your website is crucial to its functionality and user satisfaction. Update your website with these steps:

1. Back up your site often to avoid difficulties. This helps speed up site restoration and reduce downtime.

2. Update Software and Plugins: Upgrade your website software and plugins to keep it secure and up-to-date. Check for and apply updates regularly.

3. Add Fresh Content: Update your website regularly to keep it fresh and entertaining. New content includes blog posts, articles, photographs, videos, and more.

4. Fix Broken Links: Inspect your website for broken links regularly. Broken links affect SEO and user experience.

5. Check Website Performance: Make sure your website works well and loads swiftly by monitoring it periodically. Employ website speed testing tools to find ways to speed up your site.

6. Interact with Users: Respond to comments, emails, and other user input on your website. This can help you connect with your readers and improve their site experience.

Update and manage your website to keep it working, improve user experience, and increase traffic. To make sure you're monitoring for updates and updating your site, create a calendar and checklist.

Chapter 5

Promotion and Marketing

Traffic and online visibility depend on website marketing and promotion. To promote your website, follow these steps:

1. Search Engine Optimization (SEO): Use keywords, meta descriptions, and title tags to boost search engine ranks. This increases organic traffic.

2. Social Media Marketing: Promote your website and content on Facebook, Twitter, and LinkedIn. This can increase site traffic and followers.

3. Content Marketing: Create valuable material with a content marketing plan. This includes blog entries, videos, infographics, and more.

4. Email Marketing: Create an email list and utilize email marketing campaigns to promote your website and distribute information. This can keep your audience in mind and increase site traffic.

5. Paid Advertising: Employ Google Ads or social media ads to market your website and attract targeted traffic.

6. Work with Influencers: Get industry influencers to promote your site and share your material. This can increase site traffic and audience.

Marketing and advertising your website can boost traffic, internet presence, revenue, and conversions. To engage with your audience and promote your website across channels, create a marketing and promotion plan.

Website Marketing Strategy

A website marketing strategy entails identifying your target audience, creating a messaging strategy, and choosing the best methods to reach them. Steps to establishing a successful website marketing strategy:

1. Create Buyer Personas: Find your ideal consumer. Create demographic, pain point, and interest profiles of your target clients.

2. Strategize: Create a targeted message that addresses your audience's problem concerns. This can help you distinguish your brand from the competitors.

3. Choose Marketing Channels: Choose the finest methods to reach your target audience. Social media, email, content, sponsored advertising, and others are examples.

4. Establish Goals and Objectives: Define your marketing goals, such as increasing website traffic, prospects, or sales. Establish channel-specific goals.

5. Create a Content Marketing Strategy: Create blog articles, videos, infographics, and other targeted content. This might boost site traffic and demonstrate your industry authority.

6. Promote your website on Facebook, Twitter, and LinkedIn. This can increase site traffic and followers.

7. Use Email Marketing: Create an email list and promote your website and content using email marketing campaigns. This can keep your audience in mind and increase site traffic.

Using these steps, you can create a thorough marketing strategy to attract your target audience, boost traffic to your website, and meet your company goals. To achieve success, assess and adapt your marketing approach regularly.

Social Media Website Promotion

Social networking can boost website traffic. Social media tips for website promotion:

1. Choose the Correct Platforms: Focus on your target audience's most popular social media channels. This might help you reach the correct people and maximize social media efforts.

2. Share Your Content: Post blog articles, infographics, and videos on social media. This might boost site traffic and demonstrate your industry authority.

3. Interact with Followers: Respond to comments, like and share content, and ask for feedback. This can boost brand awareness and community.

4. Employ Paid Advertising: Utilize social media paid advertising to reach more people and increase website traffic.

Social media advertising is powerful because it can target people by age, geography, and hobbies.

5. Conduct Contests and Giveaways: Use social media to promote your website and communicate with fans. This boosts brand awareness and site traffic.

Cross-promote your social media profiles on your website and vice versa. This can boost social media followers and website traffic.

Social networking can help you reach more people, establish a following, and increase website traffic. Review your social media data often to identify which strategies work best and change your plan.

Content Creation for Traffic

High-quality content is a great method to increase website visitors. Traffic-driving content development and distribution tips:

1. Employ keyword research and consumer feedback to find audience-relevant themes. Create content that solves their problems.

2. Employ Several Formats: Appeal to different learning styles and preferences by using multiple content forms. Use blog entries, videos, infographics, podcasts, and eBooks.

3. Search Engine Optimization: Use keywords, meta descriptions, and tags to optimize your content for search engines. This boosts search rankings and site visitors.

4. Share Your Content on Social Media: Share your content on social media to get more visitors. Share your material on platforms where your audience is active.

5. Guest Post on Other Sites: Guest writing on other industry websites can increase site traffic and exposure. Author bios should link to your webpage.

Employ email marketing to promote your content to subscribers. This can increase site traffic and generate a devoted following.

7. Repurpose Your Content: Use different formats to reach more people. Make a movie or infographic from a blog post.

High-quality content can boost website traffic, establish your authority, and cultivate a dedicated following. Review your analytics often to find the best content forms and themes and change your strategy.

Website Promotion

Online advertising is crucial to business promotion and website traffic. Online website promotion:

1. Pay-Per-Click (PPC) Advertising: You pay only when someone clicks on your ad on search engines and other websites. PPC advertising is prevalent on Google and Facebook.

2. Social media advertising: You can place ads on Facebook, Instagram, Twitter, and LinkedIn. Demographics, hobbies, and habits can target audiences.

3. Display Advertising: Websites, blogs, and other online platforms display ads. Millions of websites accept Google Display Network advertisements.

4. Influencer Marketing: Social media influencers promote your products and services. Influencers can expand your social media reach.

5. Email marketing: Sending subscribers promotional emails. Email marketing can promote new items, sales, and website traffic.

6. Content marketing: Provide valuable material for your audience. Content marketing can increase website traffic and brand authority.

7. Affiliate marketing: Partnering with other businesses to promote your products or services. Each affiliate sale earns a commission.

Combining these online advertising tactics can increase website traffic and audience reach. Track your results and make adjustments to reach your goals.

Conclusion

Each business that wants to grow online needs a website. A website requires planning, design, development, optimization for search engines and mobile devices, maintenance, and promotion.

This tutorial will help you build a website that fits your company goals, engages your target audience, and grows your business online. Maintain your website, watch and analyze traffic, and use internet advertising to promote and drive traffic.

A well-designed and optimized website may establish your firm as a respectable and trustworthy authority in your sector, generate more leads and sales, and contribute to long-term digital success.

Website Upkeep and Optimization

Maintaining and optimizing your website keeps it current, safe, and working well. Reasons for continuing maintenance and optimization:

1. Security: Frequent upgrades and maintenance protect your website from cyberattacks. Updating software, plugins, and security measures are essential.

2. User Experience: Website maintenance and optimization can assist in ensuring a smooth user experience. This involves checking website speed, repairing broken links, and evaluating functionality.

3. SEO: SEO requires constant maintenance and adjustment. Update website content, optimize metadata and tags, and track keyword ranks and traffic.

4. Brand Image: Your website represents your brand; therefore, keep it updated. Maintenance and optimization help you retain a professional brand image.

5. Competitive Advantage: Update and optimize your website to remain competitive and ahead clients coming back.

Website upkeep and optimization are vital for long-term business success. To keep your website running well, schedule regular maintenance, monitor performance and security, and make improvements as needed.

Business Website Success Strategies

Business website tips:

1. Set your website's aims and objectives before developing it. Features and design components will depend on your goals.

2. Know your audience: Knowing your audience can help you design a website that suits their wants and interests. While designing and writing website content, consider demographics, interests, and behaviors.

3. Establish a strong brand identity: Your website should match your business's messaging, style, and tone. Brand your logo, color scheme, and graphic elements.

4. Make your website design basic and user-friendly: Visitors will locate what they need faster if your website is easy to use. Avoid confusing layouts and mobile-optimized websites.

5. Optimize your website for search engines: This will help potential customers find you by ranking higher in search results.

Increase website visibility with appropriate keywords, meta tags, and descriptions.

6. Update and manage your website often to keep it secure, up-to-date, and running well. Fixing broken links, upgrading software and plugins, and adding new information.

7. Drive traffic and visibility to your website via social media, email marketing, and other online advertising.

Using these guidelines, you can build a successful company website that engages your target audience, reflects your brand, and helps you reach your goals.